BRITISH
ARCHITECTURAL
STYLES

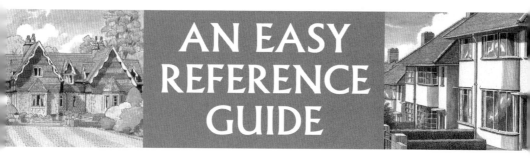

AN EASY
REFERENCE
GUIDE

Trevor Yorke

COUNTRYSIDE BOOKS
NEWBURY BERKSHIRE

First published 2008
© Trevor Yorke, 2008
Reprinted 2009, 2012, 2014, 2016, 2018

COUNTRYSIDE BOOKS
3 Catherine Road
Newbury, Berkshire

To view our complete range of books,
please visit us at
www.countrysidebooks.co.uk

ISBN 978 1 84674 082 4

Designed by Peter Davies, Nautilus Design

Produced by The Letterworks Ltd., Reading
Printed by Holywell Press, Oxford

 # Contents

Introduction

Houses are more than homes. They can be outward expressions of the owner's aspirations, a reflection of the local geology, or a canvas for the latest fashion to appear on. En masse they can form imposing terraces and squares which characterise a town. Medieval York, Georgian Bath, Regency Brighton and Victorian Manchester are just some of the places distinguished by their housing. Yet, where do you start if you wish to understand the immense and bewildering range of structures and styles? This book simply uses drawings to illustrate the principal changes through the ages which can help you date and appreciate houses. At the end is a glossary, timechart and a list of other books in this range should you wish to take the subject further.

There are a few general points which are worth mentioning before looking in detail at period houses. The 450 years or so covered in this book have seen immense changes in bricks and mortar. When Henry Tudor became King of England in 1485 most of the few million population still lived off the land, in homes which were only designed to stand for a generation or two. The houses which generally survive today from then and up to the 18th century are the finer quality urban and country houses, most of which were vernacular, made from local materials by masons and carpenters who passed their knowledge down from one generation to the next. There were, however, underlying structural and decorative changes which are common across most of the country rather than just one region and the early chapters focus upon these.

In this pre industrial age, fashion took time to spread, so a new style in London may not appear in the far flung reaches of the country until fifty years later. Few also could afford to completely replace their house, so the latest fashion was applied over an older structure. Dates on the outside, especially of 18th-century buildings, are often of the refit and not the original structure beneath. Interiors change regularly and few original ones survive, but more permanent fixtures like stairs and fireplaces can be found so it is these which are generally shown at the end of each chapter.

Housing makes dramatic changes from the 18th century as tighter regulations, improved transporting of goods and ideas, increased wealth and a booming population resulted in standardisation of form, widespread availability of materials, and national styles. Vernacular housing is replaced by uniform brick and stone structures, with the latest decoration applied to its exterior. A wider range of houses survives from this period, including smaller terraces built for an emerging middle class, and the illustrations in the later chapters reflect this broader diversity of building.

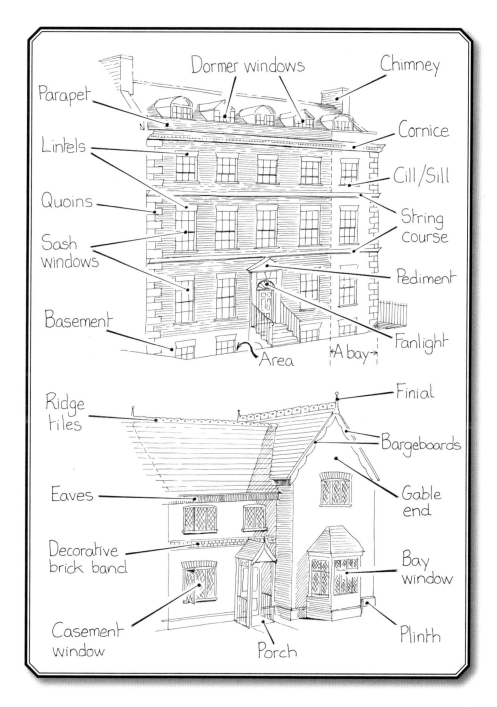

Dormer windows — Chimney

Parapet

Cornice

Lintels

Cill/Sill

Quoins

String course

Sash windows

Pediment

Basement

Fanlight

Area

A bay

Finial

Ridge tiles

Bargeboards

Eaves

Gable end

Decorative brick band

Bay window

Casement window

Porch

Plinth

Chapter ❶

Tudor House Style

1485 - 1560

Hampton Court, Surrey: *This most notable of Tudor houses was built by Cardinal Wolsey but fell into Henry VIII's hands, who set about expanding it into a royal palace. This gatehouse incorporates all the fashionable features of the day, including red brick with stone dressing, diaper patterns, oriel windows and prominent chimneys, yet still retains medieval details like the crenellations along the top and the courtyard layout.*

The **Tudor period** was one of great change, improving fortunes and notorious monarchs! The feudal system, cornerstone of medieval society, had broken down as a population, halved by the Black Death and subsequent periodic outbreaks of plague, sought greater freedom and opportunities, with families originally from a poor background acquiring land and wealth over generations to become yeomen farmers, merchants, or even gentry. The creation of the Church of England and the Dissolution of the Monasteries under Henry VIII created huge social upheaval and resulted in a large amount of land being granted to the King's favourites, although doubts over the permanence of his actions meant few did much with their new properties in this period. It is the houses, large and small, of these newly successful families, alongside those of the existing landed classes, which survive today.

Structure

Tudor towns and cities were generally small, with houses set upon thin plots of land with a narrow frontage overlooking the street. Villages were dominated by the manor house and two-storey farmhouses while around them the majority of the rural population was housed in simple buildings of timber, mud or rubble. These were often shared with the livestock and may have lasted a few hundred years or just a generation, but only survive today as raised platforms in deserted villages. The houses of the successful and wealthy were generally one room deep because the weight of the roof structure limited greater width, and there was little attention to outward display and style. Most large houses were asymmetrical arrangements of buildings looking inwards upon a courtyard. The urban houses of merchants and tradesmen often had a shop, warehouse or workshop on the lower storey with accommodation jettied above.

Exterior Style

The gentry had been little concerned with the arts, their wealth was spent embellishing the House of God to secure passage through purgatory rather than in decorating their own residences. It was later in this period before they became aware of the artistic flowering of the Renaissance, only for contact with this new flow of European culture to be severed by the Reformation. The finest timber-framed houses featured close studding (tightly fitted vertical members) or had decorative timber patterns set in the panels to demonstrate the owner's wealth. Many, especially in towns, had jetties overhanging the lower floor, a status symbol as much as a way of creating extra space. Bricks were typically red, often with stone dressing for the windows and quoins (corner stones) and diaper patterns (diagonal crosses) formed out of over-burnt dark grey bricks.

Wealden House:

A popular style of house in the south and east of the country was the Wealden House. Built for the lesser gentry and farmers, it had a recessed open hall in the centre with two-storey cross wings at either end, all under a single roof.

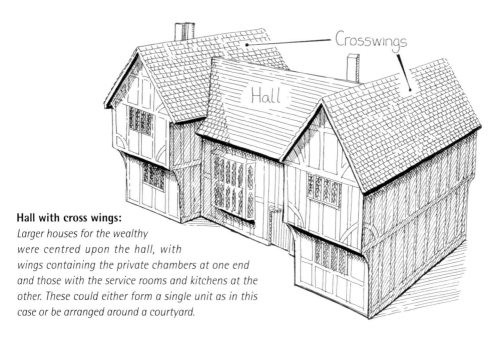

Hall with cross wings:
Larger houses for the wealthy
were centred upon the hall, with
wings containing the private chambers at one end
and those with the service rooms and kitchens at the
other. These could either form a single unit as in this
case or be arranged around a courtyard.

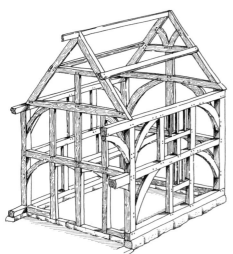

Box frame: A box-framed house stripped of
its wattle and daub infill to reveal its basic
structure. The wealthier owners in this period
fitted decorative or close studded timbers in
the wall panels.

Urban house with jetty: Urban houses were
usually timber framed with jetties providing
extra room on upper floors and higher status.
Some had the gable end facing the street; in
others the roof ran parallel to it.

Close studding and decorative panels: *Examples of close studding (left) which was popular in the south and east and decorative framing (right) which was more usually found in some western counties. This excessive use of timber was a sign of wealth.*

Brick with stone dressing and diaper patterns: *A close-up of a brick wall with long Tudor bricks and a lighter coloured stone dressing. The darker ends of burnt bricks form the crosses which make a diaper pattern on the upper half while below they are laid in an English Bond, alternate courses of the short ends (headers) and long sides (stretchers), which were all popular in this period. Brick had been reintroduced into this country in the 14th century and was popular in the east and south of the country.*

Crenellations, machiolations and arrow loops: *Features from castles like crenellations (left), machicolations (top), and arrow loops (right) were still fitted to most major houses if only for decorative effect.*

Chimneys: *Fireplaces were a new luxury fitting and tall decorative brick chimneys were fitted above to display the fact.*

Timber mullion window: *Most windows in this period originally had no glazing. The openings were divided by vertical mullions with shutters or oiled cloth behind to keep the worst of the weather out.*

Oriel window: *Oriel windows projected from an upper storey and were a common form of display on larger houses, often above gateways or important entrances.*

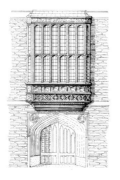

Bay window: *Bay windows stretched from the ground up and were often fitted at the lord's end of the great hall to cast extra light and give a clear view of who was at the entrance.*

Stone window with label mould: *In the finest houses stone framed windows with decorative carving at the top (tracery) and diamond-leaded glass could be fitted. The raised hat shaped feature along the top called a label or hood mould was a popular feature.*

Door with decorative spandrels: *Important doorways to larger houses usually had a flat, four-centred arched opening. The triangular gaps above this, called spandrels, were often decorative in this period.*

Interior Style

The most important members of society had numerous estates and spent much of the year travelling between their houses, carting even some of their furniture along with them. The interior of even the largest house was fairly spartan by modern standards. The large communal hall of the medieval period was still common but many houses had a ceiling inserted and smaller private rooms fitted above, giving new opportunities for decoration. This was only possible due to the development of the chimney as open hearths in the middle of the room were replaced by fireplaces. Walls could be painted with decorative patterns, covered with cloth hangings or, increasingly later in the period, panelled in. These were wooden square frames, either over the lower part or the full height of the room, with fielded or linenfold panels set in them.

Large fireplace: *A large inset fireplace with four-centred arch opening and heraldic decoration above.*

Timber panelling: *Square-framed timber panelling was fitted around the best room or along the screen at the end of the hall. This example shows the linenfold pattern which was a popular decorative effect in this period. Note the bottom edge of each frame was a plain chamfer making it easy to dust.*

The hall: *The principal element of any large house was the hall, a large central space open to the rafters in which the owner and his household ate and slept. Behind the dais would have been access to the private chambers, while at the opposite end from where the owner sat would have been doors leading to the service rooms and a kitchen which was usually detached as a fire precaution. As fireplaces became more common during this period, a ceiling was often inserted across these halls to create more rooms upstairs.*

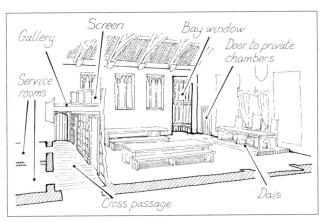

Chapter ②

Elizabethan and Jacobean House Style

1560 - 1660

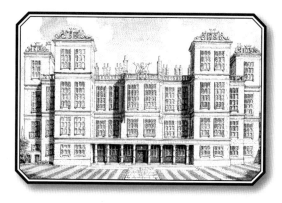

Hardwick Hall, Derbyshire: *Built in the 1590s for Bess of Hardwick, probably by the leading designer of his time, Robert Smythson, Hardwick Hall is notable for 'more glass than wall'. It was radically different from early Tudor houses with a symmetrical layout, the hall relegated to an entrance room, state rooms on the upper floors, and masses of windows.*

A rising population, growing incomes and an increased confidence that the religious changes made under Henry VIII were permanent became driving forces behind what has been termed the Great Rebuilding. Those who had been granted monastic estates under the old king now began knocking down their medieval lodgings and erected imposing new mansions, while others rebuilt on the possibility of attracting a royal visit (Elizabeth built no new palaces and relied upon her subjects to accommodate her during the summer months when she left London). In the town and country the lesser gentry, merchants and farmers built timber-framed houses, the more closely-packed vertical timber member, decorative woodwork, glass windows and jettied storeys, the better!

Structure

Masonry and brick began to appear further down the social scale with large manor and farm houses two or three storeys high often laid out in an 'E' or 'H' shaped plan. The Elizabethans loved hidden messages in their architecture and the layout and detailing of buildings could indicate an allegiance to the queen ('E'-shaped plan) or something prohibited (triangular, representing the Trinity). The majority of the population still lived in simple one-storey houses and although some improved their situation perhaps by removing livestock from inside and creating another room, most would not benefit until a later period. Timber framing was still popular in the north and west of the country although it was falling from favour elsewhere.

Exterior style

The Renaissance (the rebirth of classical art and architecture) still found its way into the design of many new buildings. Large houses now had a symmetrical façade and rather than looking inwards upon a courtyard they faced outwards, displaying the wealth of the owner through large numbers of glass windows. Classical details like columns and pediments were used but with little knowledge of the rules of proportion, so they were simply applied or stacked as decoration. Chimneys became a standard fitting on the better class of house. The accession to the throne of James I in 1603 ('Jacobean' is from *Jacobus*, the Latin for *James*) brought in a taste for Dutch gables and cupolas.

Little Moreton Hall, Cheshire: *Most houses were still timber-framed in this period, the finest examples as here at Little Moreton featuring decorative panels, numerous jetties and masses of patterned glass.*

House plans: *'H' and 'E'-shaped plans with roughly symmetrical fronts and tall narrow gabled wings and porches facing the approach were distinctive of this period (top). Some of the finest houses were still built around a courtyard with, in the early 17th century, Dutch gables, cupolas, ogee-capped towers and prominent horizontal string courses running around the building being fashionable (bottom).*

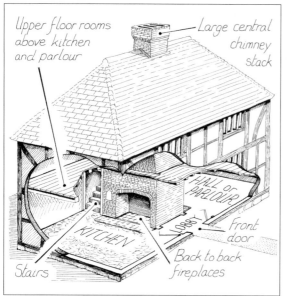

Upper floor rooms above kitchen and parlour — Large central chimney stack — HALL or PARLOUR — Front door — LOBBY — Back to back fireplaces — KITCHEN — Stairs

Axial stacks: *A popular layout for more modest houses in the south and east during this period and slightly later elsewhere was to position the chimney stack centrally, with fireplaces facing into the two ground floor rooms. The entrance door opened into one side and the stairs were usually fitted on the other.*

Decorative beams: *Important timber-framed urban houses could be finished with decorative panels and jetties, with the main horizontal beam moulded rather than plain and in some cases supported with carved brackets.*

Hatfield House, Hertfordshire: *Dutch gables, cupolas, twinned columns flanking porches, and semi-circular doorways were Classical details which found their way onto some of the finest houses.*

Decorative windows: *Windows with patterned glass were popular in the finest houses, although diamond-shaped leaded panes were more common. Many originally had a central thin metal stanchion fitted behind as a security measure and to help strengthen the fragile leaded pane. It was common for only one of the lights to be hinged so it could swing open for ventilation (bottom centre).*

Mullioned and transomed windows: *Larger mullioned and transomed windows could be long or tall with numerous lights (the single opening between mullions or transoms into which a set of panes were fixed). Some had smaller windows flanking on either side. It was still common for a label or hood mould to run over the top of these windows.*

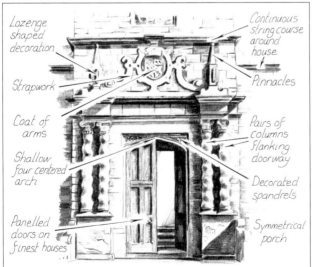

Doorways: *An entrance to a large house with labels of some of the features which can be found from the late 16th and early 17th century. Although most doors were formed of planks and battens, some of the finest Jacobean houses had richly decorated panelled doors.*

15

Chimneys: *Chimneys continued to be tall and thin, arranged in groups of two or more. There was a wider variety of forms on the finest houses, including cylindrical (left) and later more rectangular types often with jetties of brick at the top (right).*

Doors: *On many houses four-centred arched doorways and mullioned windows were still fitted. These are more likely now to have moulding around them and diamond-leaded glass. The door was usually a plank and batten type with vertical fillets covering the joints and long strap hinges.*

Strapwork: *Flat, plain decorative bands in geometric shapes and raised just above the surface of walls and known as strapwork were a distinctive feature of late 16th and early 17th century houses. Parapets with open geometric shapes or the name of the owner were also popular at this time.*

Porches: *Tall, narrow porches with Classical decorations stacked upon each other were common on larger houses, as with this rather clumsy assortment! Semi-circular arched doorways were also popular for the important entrances to this class of house.*

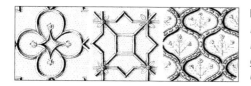

Plaster ceiling: *The finest houses might have a plaster ceiling fixed off the beams. Elizabethan examples tended to have geometric patterns (left and middle) which became deeper in the Jacobean period (right).*

Interior Style

The sudden change in the appearance of many of the new houses in this period was mirrored inside. The old medieval great hall declined in importance and began to be replaced by individual rooms with a specific role, and many of these new principal rooms had ceilings with exposed beams, but the finest had plaster decoration. As there were now important upstairs rooms, the stairs rose to prominence, coming out of the corner and, by the Jacobean period, were a central feature, with richly carved newel posts and balusters. Fireplaces were still a luxury fitting and were a key feature in rooms, often with a heavily decorated overmantel above. Wood panelling was still the choice covering for the important rooms, square with plain or geometric patterns being popular in the Elizabethan period and increasingly classically proportioned with columns in the Jacobean age.

Beamed ceilings: *Most ceilings at this date had the beams, joists, and boards of the above floor exposed. The edges of the main timber pieces were chamfered or, as in this case, with a moulding finishing in a decorative stop. Finer examples might have a central boss, painted boards inserted between the beams or the joists arranged at different angles to form a chequerboard pattern.*

Stairs: *A well staircase from a large house with (A) risers, (B) treads, (C) the newel post, (D) balusters, (E) a closed string (with the risers and treads running into it). A dog gate (F) was still to be found in some houses to stop them getting up to the private chambers. Jacobean houses were noted for their highly elaborately carved newel posts, finials and balusters.*

Classical panelling: *In large Jacobean houses elaborate Classically proportioned panelling with columns, arches and strapwork could be found.*

Fireplaces: *Important fireplaces in this period often had decorative overmantels above them with rich carving, as in this example. The fireplace opening itself tended to be simple with a square or flat four-centred arch opening and chamfered edges.*

Splat balusters: *More modest houses sometimes had balusters cut from a plank (splat balusters) rather than turned or carved, which usually had a mirrored profile tapering from top to bottom.*

Panelling: *Square panelling was still popular in the finest houses, now with either plain, fielded (C) or geometric patterns. A frieze along the top was common with arcading (A) and moulding around the upper and side edges (B) and plain at the bottom (E) for ease of dusting. Strapwork could often be found for decorative details (D).*

Chapter ③

Restoration House Style

1660 - 1714

Belton House, Lincs: *Built in the late 1680s, it has two roughly equal height storeys and a central triangular pediment, with oval windows and a decorative feature within. It also has a hipped roof, plain rectangular chimneys, a balustrade and cupola along the top, and dormer windows with alternate arched and triangular pediments, all of which are characteristic of the period.*

This period of great change began with the ascent to the throne of Charles II after years of exile in Holland and France during the Civil War and Protectorate. Six years later the Great Fire of London ripped the heart out of the capital. The huge scale of the disaster forced the authorities into creating legislation which would ensure it would not be repeated by controlling the structure and materials of new houses, regulations which applied to London but were gradually adopted elsewhere. Many builders no longer erected single buildings for a client, but were speculators who took the risk of erecting houses in the hope of finding tenants and a profit. Most, however, only built a few at a time, and slight differences in alignment or style in a long row of houses can indicate where one builder finished and another started.

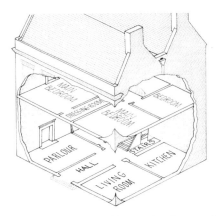

Double piled house: *More modest houses of the successful urbanite or farmer could also be double piled, often with the stairs at the rear and a small fanlight above the front door to illuminate the central hall now there were no outside walls for windows to be fitted in.*

Structure

The large houses of the aristocracy and increasingly the lesser gentry were double piled, that is, they were two rooms deep in a single rectangular block rather than one room deep wrapped around a courtyard. The steep pitch which roof coverings demanded meant that these had to be covered by hipped roofs in a ring or two parallel pitched roofs with distinctive twin gables on the side elevation. The two main floors were also usually of similar height in this period rather than made taller to emphasise the most important rooms. These new houses were now built in stone or brick, the latter being more readily available and cheaper and now found further north and west. Some timber-framed houses were still built in certain areas although brick was often used for plinths and chimneys.

Exterior Style

The followers of Charles II and later William of Orange brought with them a taste for Classical architecture Dutch-style. Jolly, stout red-brick houses with white cornices, highlighted quoins, hipped roofs with dormer windows and cupolas were fashionable. This Dutch style worked its way down to more modest houses and terraces while at the same time a new monumental and flamboyant style which had developed in Italy in the first half of the 17th century became fashionable on the finest houses. Baroque (a name coined by a later generation as a slur meaning 'mis-shaped pearl') was distinguished by large-scale sprawling houses with flamboyant monumental decoration and was particularly suited to places like Blenheim Palace and Castle Howard.

Brick bonding: *The way bricks were laid in walls began to change, with Flemish replacing English Bond. Soft orange/red bricks known as rubbers were used as they could be sanded down to make fine jointed decoration to contrast with the main walls. Stone dressing was used with brick for a similar effect.*

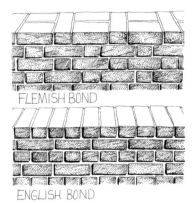

FLEMISH BOND

ENGLISH BOND

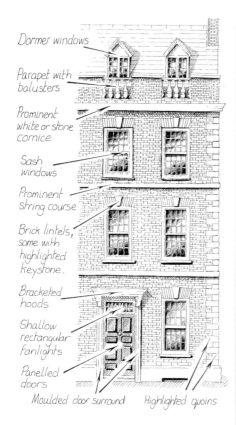

Labels on the left house:
- Dormer windows
- Parapet with balusters
- Prominent white or stone cornice
- Sash windows
- Prominent string course
- Brick lintels, some with highlighted keystone.
- Bracketed hoods
- Shallow rectangular fanlights
- Panelled doors
- Moulded door surround
- Highlighted quoins

Labels on the right house:
- Alternate triangular and segmental arched pediments on dormer windows
- Hipped roof
- White cornice
- Sash or cross windows Flush with wall
- Flemish bond brickwork
- Plain string course
- Hooded doorway with rectangular fanlight

Terrace house: *A medium-sized house dating from the reign of Queen Anne (1701-1714) with labels of characteristic features from this period.*

Dutch style house: *A characteristic stout red-brick house with two equal height storeys and an attic, dating from the late 17th and early 18th century, with labels of its period details. The projecting string course, often of contrasting stone, ran horizontally around in place of the separate hood moulds over individual windows which had been popular before.*

Winslow Hall façade: *A large detached house by Sir Christopher Wren dating from 1700. It features stone quoins and finer quality bricks around the windows and a segmental arched pediment above the door. The round window within the large central triangular pediment is distinctive of this period.*

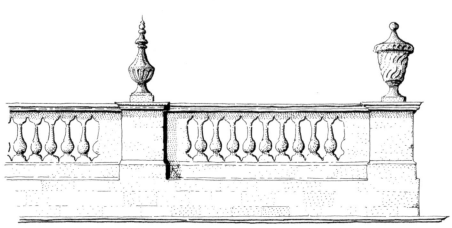

Baroque style features: *Details from large Baroque style houses.*

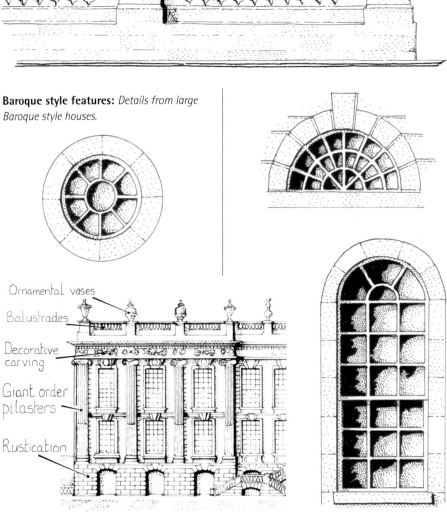

Ornamental vases

Balustrades

Decorative carving

Giant order pilasters

Rustication

Cross windows: *Cross windows with a single mullion and a transom set slightly above centre and rectangular rather than diamond shaped lights became popular on the finest houses as their tall dimensions suited Classical proportions. These were often replaced by sash windows at a later date.*

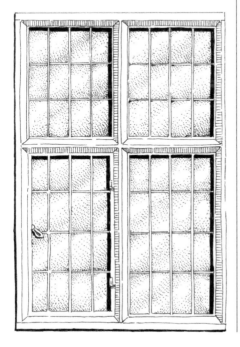

Sash windows: *From the 1680s sash windows became available. Two frames (sashes) divided by glazing bars, typically creating 9, 12 or 16 lights in each one, were set in a wooden box. At this date just the lower sash moved up or down and the box was flush or slightly projecting from the exterior wall.*

Pediments: *Pediments above doors and windows could be either triangular or segmental or often a mix of both. Stone or white deep-set examples on dormer windows were distinctive of this period.*

Doors: *These were panelled in the finest examples, often with six or eight panels of varying size. Above was usually fitted a shallow rectangular fanlight divided up with vertical mullions, some added later making the door below seem rather squat. Most doors, however, were still plank and batten with mouldings applied to make them look similar to panelled versions.*

Hoods: *Richly carved door hoods are a distinctive feature of the late 17th and early 18th centuries. Some were just rectangular or segmental arched projections on shallow brackets but others were prominent arched hoods with shell patterns or rich carving beneath.*

Interior styles

In the finest interiors naturalistic and intricate wood carvings by master craftsmen like Grinling Gibbons complemented panelled walls with the Classical arrangement of tall upper and short lower panels in the finest interiors. The important rooms had deep recessed ceilings divided into panels by decorated ribs with a large central (usually oval) piece containing a painting or moulding. In the largest houses these state apartments were arranged in a straight line with double doors leading from one into another, a distinctive feature of the period called an enfilade. Stairs had beautifully carved newel posts and balusters and were now usually open beneath, with the underside sometimes decorated. A distinctive form of decoration from the period is bolection moulding, which protrudes outwards the nearer it gets to the centre of the feature it is surrounding, like a door or fireplace.

Fireplace: *Most fireplace and door surrounds used the distinctive bolection moulding which was more pronounced on the edge of the opening and shallower further away. Iron firebacks to reflect heat back into the room were popular, especially featuring the Royal Coat of Arms.*

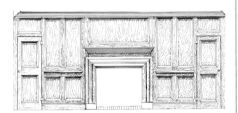

Wall panelling: *The finest interiors were still panelled in wood, now laid out with large upper and shorter lower panels to suit the Classical style of house. Rich intricate carving by master craftsmen like Grinling Gibbons usually accompanied this.*

Stairs: *Richly decorated wooden stairways, now open beneath, were still popular in the largest houses, with the carved balusters now typically a vase shape with the broader part on the lower section rather than the opposite way round as had been used in the early 17th century. Barley twist balusters (left) were also popular.*

Chapter ❹

Georgian House Style

1714 - 1790

Chiswick House, London: *The Georgian period is distinguished by refined, elegant buildings which appear plain compared with the ornamental Baroque which preceded it. One of the first buildings to break the mould was Chiswick House, built in the 1720s by the 3rd Earl of Burlington who championed the architecture of Ancient Rome as reinterpreted by Andrea Palladio. This Palladian style was filtered down to shape the villas and terraces of the period.*

The 18th century saw the meeting of the medieval and modern worlds, where the majority of people still lived and worked on the land but improvements in agriculture and industry were bringing new benefits, mainly to the aristocracy who lavished their wealth upon country houses and urban properties. Alongside them a new middle class began to grow and London expanded rapidly, with tall Georgian terraces lining roads and squares built to house them, while ports, industrial towns and fashionable resorts like Bath also developed. The mass of the population were still left to struggle – some might have new housing as enclosure of common land and the building of parks around country houses resited villages, while others who were uprooted could find better pay in the growing industrial towns and cities.

Large Georgian houses: *Examples like this tend to have an elegant but plain façade with restrained decoration and a portico or pedimented door surround as its key feature. By the 1770s when this house was built the ground floor was often raised with steps up to the door so more light could access the half basement below.*

Structure

Large, symmetrically fronted double pile houses continued to be built, although there were subtle changes to the layout as owners looked to keep a more respectable distance between the family and the servants and an ever larger and more impressive suite of rooms for entertaining was required. Most new houses were urban terraces, divided into classes and regulated by legislation, their façades shaped as much by a need to reduce the fire risk as by rules of Classical proportions. The smaller houses of the working population, for the first time, survive today from this period, although even the humble rural cottage or almshouse, or urban two up, two down were built for the fortunate or most successful from this class.

Exterior Style

A new style became dominant during the first half of the 18th century as the flamboyant Baroque was replaced by the more subdued and refined Palladian architecture. Named after the 16th-century Italian architect Palladio, who reinterpreted Roman buildings, it relied upon correct use of size, proportion and arrangement of parts for impact and used the form of the temple from the ancient world with rusticated bases and rows of columns across entrances (porticoes) as a key part of the design. This was watered down to shape the new terraces which were strikingly plain but elegant. In the second half of the century a new generation of architects, such as Robert Adam, were inspired by discoveries from the Ancient World and used more decoration upon still essentially Palladian forms of building.

Palladian terraces: *A large Palladian terrace, with labels of key features.*

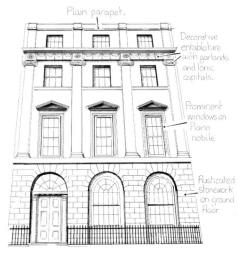

Classes of terrace: *The 1667 Rebuilding Act for London and the 1774 Building Act categorised urban houses into different rates. These were defined by the value of the property and its total floor area (sq ft).*

Early façade: *A large early Georgian terrace with labels of some of the period features. It was common at this date for the basement to be fully sunk below the house with the front door flush with the pavement.*

Later façade: *A modest-sized later terrace, with labels of some of the period features. Houses of this class and above generally had a half basement, with steps leading up to an elevated front door and an open area in front to access the service rooms below.*

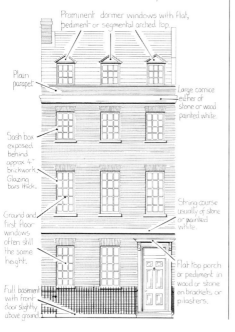

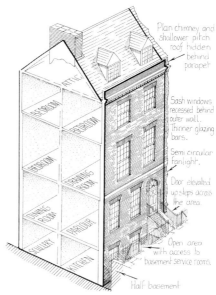

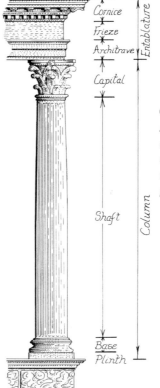

Capitals: Corinthian, Ionic and Doric:
Roman forms of the Classical orders were used on Georgian houses until the latter part of the century. The three principal ones were the Corinthian (left), Ionic (centre) and Doric (right). The Composite merged the Corinthian and Ionic in one, and the Tuscan was similar in form to the Doric.

Column:
An elevation of a Classical column, with labels of its parts.

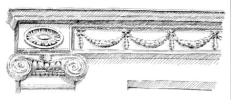

Adam style details: *Robert Adam was the most influential architect of the late 18th century, using delicate and shallow surface decoration to enliven the Palladian form of house. He also broke up their rather austere façades with Venetian windows, wide doorways flanked by columns or thin windows and large semi-circular fanlights above.*

Rustication: *The lower floors of many houses were highlighted by rusticated masonry (or simulated in render). This could be smooth (left) with 'V'-shaped channels, vermiculated (centre) with curvy worm tracks, or cyclopean or rock faced (right). This was designed to look like the bases of temples upon which the Palladian style had been based.*

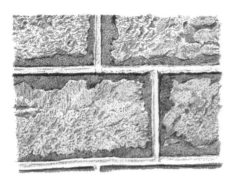

Tuck pointing: *Fine jointed brickwork was the sign of quality, so to simulate it when using cheaper, rougher edged bricks tuck pointing was used. The mortar (darker irregular areas) was coloured to match the brick and then a fine bead of white lime putty was inserted to give the impression of fine joints.*

Fanlights: *Fanlights which cast light down the long narrow halls were distinctive of the period. Earlier types tended to be rectangular with a simple pattern made out of wood or iron (top), later examples were semi-circular, with more intricate patterns formed from cast iron.*

Doorways: *The six-panelled door was dominant on houses although there were some decorative variations (left). Larger houses could have elaborate door surrounds. The Gibbs surround (left) was popular early in the period, while pedimented types with engaged columns and semi-circular fanlight (right) date from the second half of the century.*

Rainwater trap: *Iron and lead rainwater traps and guttering were a decorative feature*

on the finest houses, with distinctive strap type brackets to secure them to the wall. Be careful with the dates cast on them, as they often refer to a renovation rather than original build of a house.

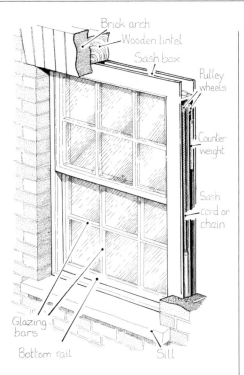

Brick arch
Wooden lintel
Sash box
Pulley wheels
Counter weight
Sash cord or chain
Glazing bars
Bottom rail
Sill

Sash window: *A drawing of a sash window, with labels of the parts. This example shows one with the sash box recessed behind the outer brick as defined in the Building Act of 1774.*

Lunette and Venetian windows: *These types of window were popular in this period, used singly or both together as in this example.*

Window regulations: *The position of the outer sash box in relation to the wall changed due to fire regulations in this period. Early examples could be exposed and flush (top) but from 1709 had to be set back four inches, and then finally recessed behind the brickwork after 1774. Other exterior wood decoration was also banned to stop the spread of fire across the front of a building.*

Interior Style

The fledgling middle classes, eager to emulate their social superiors, could now create interiors in the latest Classical styles thanks to a growing number of decorators armed with pattern books. Baroque with its opulent decoration was still popular early on, with Rococco featuring encrusted mouldings in white and gold in demand later, and more delicate Adam styles in the last years of the century. Most of this decoration was lavished upon the principal rooms in which guests were received and entertained – as soon as you retired up to bed the walls became plainer and the mouldings fewer. The most important rooms were usually the drawing and dining rooms and in this period they were increasingly positioned on the first floor, the *piano nobile*, with a higher ceiling emphasised on the exterior by the tallest windows.

Interior labels: *A Georgian principal room, with labels of parts. Plaster replaced wood panelling as the wall covering in the best houses. Wood was still used on the dado to protect it, especially in halls and dining rooms, where chairs were put up against the wall when not in use. Walls could be painted or in the finest houses covered with wallpaper, fabrics and even leather.*

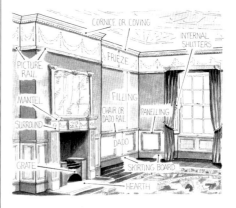

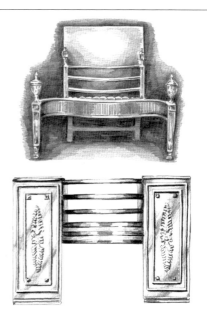

Fireplace grates: *Coal grew in popularity and availability through the century, with smaller basket grates (top and top right) to hold them compared with types for wood. Hob grates with flat upper surfaces to the sides for cooking or heating water became popular (right).*

Fireplace surrounds: *The focal point of most rooms was decorated to suit its importance, from elaborate marble, stone and hardwoods in the best rooms to simple cheaper types in bedrooms. Early ones still had the bolection moulding although this was quickly replaced by Classically styled types from the flamboyant Rococco (left) to the refined Adam style (right).*

Stairs: *Treads were cantilevered out of the wall rather than supported upon newel posts so they seem to float up. This effect was further enhanced by the use of open string stairs where the balusters rest upon the upper surface of the tread. Balusters become more delicate and are often set in twos and threes with barley twists remaining popular (top) and iron types with mahogany handrails appearing in the later 18th century (bottom).*

Ceilings: *Deep plaster mouldings (left) and flamboyant Rococco styles in white and gold were popular on the finest ceilings in the first part of the period. Later designs inspired by Robert Adam tended to be shallower patterns with delicate detailing and muted colours. Most rooms had plain ceilings with the main decorative effort going into the cornice.*

Chapter ⑤

Regency House Style

1790 - 1830

Brighton, Sussex: *Seaside resorts began to develop for the wealthy in this period, the most notable being Brighton. Straight roads and squares leading down to the seafront were packed with tall terraces coated in stucco, a render which was coloured to imitate the fashionable beige and grey stone of the time, but which also could cover up poor building (this is the period when the phrase 'jerry building' was first coined, from a nautical term for temporary rigging).*

The Regency period architecturally lasted from 1790 to 1830 (although George III's son was only Regent from 1811 to 1820) and had distinctive styles of building. These appeared not only in the booming capital, growing industrial cities and ports but also in new seaside resorts like Brighton and spa towns like Cheltenham. These were where the fashionable went to be seen and the terraces built here had balconies and bay windows from which people promenading could be viewed.

Napoleon's expeditions to Egypt and growing trade with our commercial interests abroad also produced a taste for Egyptian, Chinese and Oriental products which appear in interiors from the time and occasionally on the exterior. The improved road network and the new canals meant more mundane products like building materials could be transported across the country, lowering costs and beginning the end of vernacular housing.

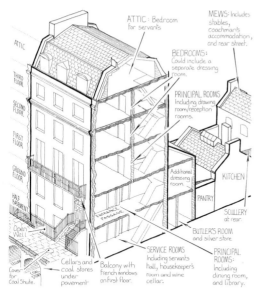

ATTIC

THIRD FLOOR

SECOND FLOOR

FIRST FLOOR

GROUND FLOOR

HALF BASEMENT

ATTIC: Bedroom for servants

MEWS: Includes stables, coachman's accommodation, and rear street.

BEDROOMS: Could include a separate dressing room.

PRINCIPAL ROOMS: Including drawing room/reception rooms.

Additional dressing room.

KITCHEN

PANTRY

SCULLERY at rear.

BUTLER'S ROOM and silver store.

Open Well

Cover for Coal Shute.

Cellars and coal stores under pavement.

Balcony with french windows on first floor.

SERVICE ROOMS Including servants hall, housekeeper's room and wine cellar.

PRINCIPAL ROOMS Including dining room, and library.

ENTRANCE PASSAGE

Large terrace: *A cut away of a large terrace from the Regency period, with labels of its parts. Note the half basement, rear extension and mews along the back as service rooms and quarters grew in scale.*

Structure

The general form of terrace houses continued as before although they generally became taller. Half-basements which raised the ground floor so it had to be accessed by steps enhanced this effect. The gradual move in the finest houses to separate servants from the family and the general demand for more specialist rooms resulted in rear extensions and service rooms and mews being built in the rear yard. In addition to the popular terrace, semi-detached and detached houses known as villas were built in the suburbs, in any number of styles although many had a distinctive shallow pitched hipped roof, which was possible now that lightweight

Welsh slate was widely available. Working class housing continued to be regionally varied and generally poor but some terraces and back to backs built in this period can still be found today.

Exterior style

Classical styles still dominated houses, with the Greek orders and forms of decoration rather than Roman now widely used. Fine-cut stone was fashionable but still expensive so brick exteriors were covered in a render called stucco which had fine lines cut in it and was then coloured beige and grey to imitate stone. The most distinctive style of the time was Gothick, a fashion which had emerged in the mid 18th century. It was based loosely on medieval castles and abbeys and was applied to the standard symmetrical houses of the time with pointed arched windows, battlements, hood moulds, and 'Y'-shaped tracery. The Napoleonic Wars also instilled a patriotism which resulted in a number of large mock castles built in this period for the very rich.

Bow windows: *Window tax, applied to houses with over six or eight of them, made bay*

windows an expensive luxury. However, they were fashionable on the finest houses, at first being hexagonal in the mid-Georgian period, then semi-circular, before in the Regency period becoming a distinctive shallow bow as in this full height example with balcony.

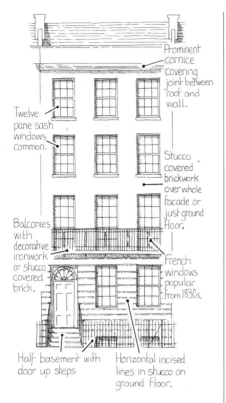

Prominent cornice covering joint between roof and wall.

Twelve pane sash windows common.

Stucco covered brickwork over whole facade or just ground floor.

Balconies with decorative ironwork or stucco covered brick.

French windows popular from 1830s.

Half basement with door up steps

Horizontal incised lines in stucco on ground floor.

Regency terrace façade: *A fashionable terrace house with labels of some of its period features.*

Gothick details: *The Regency Gothick (with a 'k' to distinguish it from the later Victorian Gothic) used wide pointed arches, battlements upon gables and medieval decoration set in stucco. Where brick was exposed in this period it was generally plain but occasionally the headers were picked out in a darker colour, as around the window with its distinctive 'Y'-shaped tracery.*

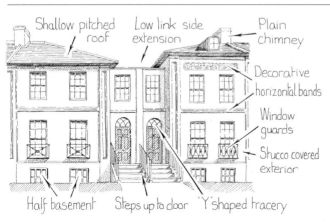

Shallow pitched roof

Low link side extension

Plain chimney

Decorative horizontal bands

Window guards

Stucco covered exterior

Half basement

Steps up to door

'Y' shaped tracery

Semis façades: *A pair of villas with labels of their fashionable features. The lower link extension with their front doors set within is a distinctive feature of the period.*

Columns: *With the accurate recording of Ancient Greek architecture from the 1760s this earlier form of Classical building began to appear here but its simple, plain forms did not become fashionable until the 1820s. The Greek Ionic (left) with its parallel scrolls and the Doric with its broad top and fluted shaft (right), however, were often used through the Regency period.*

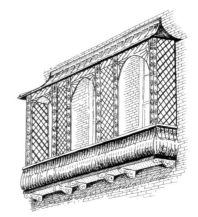

Ironwork: *With improved methods of casting especially after the Napoleonic Wars, exterior ironwork became elaborate and intricate, and was used for fanlights, railings and balconies. This example of the latter has the distinctive Chinese pagoda-style roof.*

Sash windows: *Sash windows, now with their boxes tucked away under the other brick or stone wall, had even finer glazing bars than before. These were so thin that metal was often inserted for strength.*

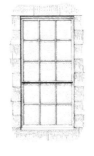

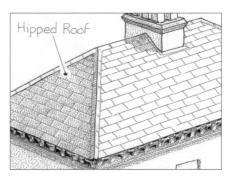

Roofs: *With the widespread availability of Welsh slate, shallow pitched roofs, hipped on semis and detached houses (above), became fashionable. A common solution for roofing terraces which kept it out of sight behind the parapet was to create a central valley with a shallow pitch to either side (left), although this is notorious for leaking.*

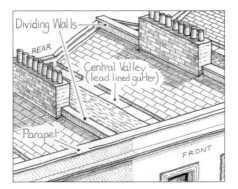

Interior Styles

The Classically-inspired styles continued to dominate Regency interiors although Gothick, Chinese and other exotic forms of decoration and detail were also used. The principal rooms were around a foot taller than in the early Georgian period and there was a fashion for having front and rear rooms open, with large windows at either end to 'let the outside in'. The dado and panelling was replaced by a picture rail in many dining rooms now that it was fashionable to keep the table and chairs permanently in the centre of the room. The dado survived in the drawing room where scattered, intimate groups of tables and chairs demanded protection for the wall.

Fireplaces: *Fireplace surrounds were generally Classically-inspired with shallow mantelpieces as the top surface was not used for display (left). The most distinctive form in this period was the fluted or reeded surround, continued around the top with distinctive bull's eyes in the corners (right).*

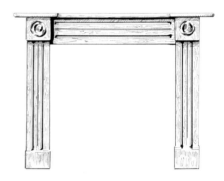

Grates: *Hob grates remained popular (right) but new register grates with an adjustable flap (the register) set in the flue to control the draw began to appear in the late 18th century (lower right) and became more widespread by the end of the period (left).*

Regency interior: *This room displays many fashionable features of the period like the bold striped wallpaper, the picture rail, reeded fireplace surround and the table and chairs permanently in the centre of the room.*

Doors: *The six-panelled door (with labels of its parts) was widespread for the front and important interior rooms. The reeded surround with bull's eyes in the corner was the most distinctive in this period.*

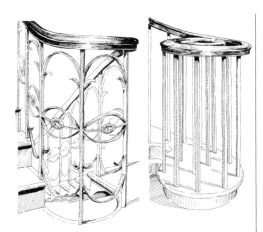

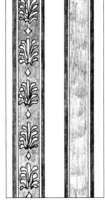

Stairs: *The finest Regency stairs were light and airy with thin iron balusters and dark wood handrails ending in spirals. Some had skylights fitted above to illuminate the stair well.*

Wallpaper: *Wallpaper remained expensive and handmade. Classically-styled papers remained popular, but Chinese-inspired designs (left) and bold stripes (right) were distinctive of the period.*

Chapter ⑥

Victorian House Style

1830 - 1900

Leek, Staffs: *Industry dominated the new towns and cities with factories and mills becoming confined to single larger sites. Around these, developed streets of housing, occasionally as at Saltaire and Port Sunlight planned as a single estate, more typically a piecemeal development, with only a few houses built in one go and often by different builders. The slight difference in alignment and style of these examples shows that they were erected at different times.*

The Victorian period is seen today as a time of industrial progress, engineering marvels and imperial expansion. Yet, despite this glorious image, growth was far more periodic and the times more turbulent than it would appear. The wealth generated began to be spread through society unlike in previous generations, but the aristocracy, shored up by wealthy industrialists keen to join their ranks, were still in control and many spent their fortunes on their country estates.

The middle classes were growing in numbers and influence and they too displayed their aspirations upon their suburban terraces and villas. For the first time the lot of the working classes gradually began to improve despite poverty, disease and no guarantees of employment. Most could expect to live in a house with around four rooms by the time Queen Victoria died in 1901 rather than the single one they all had to squeeze into when she had ascended the throne in 1837.

Structure

The finest houses were shaped by new domestic revival styles and many became sprawling asymmetrical arrangements in contrast to imposing themselves on the landscape. Houses in town centres were restricted for space and the large terrace changed little in form other than to lose its basement as conditions for servants improved. Suburban detached houses benefited from cheaper land costs and were now set back from the road, hidden behind walls and gardens, as Victorians sought privacy. Middle and working class terraces and villas (the latter name being applied to gradually smaller houses) became taller and with additional rooms usually accommodated in a new rear

Gothic mansion: *A large house dating from the 1860s in the fashionable red-brick Gothic, with an asymmetrical composition, towers and turrets, and diaper patterns and stone dressing in the walls.*

extension. Terraces also tended to have their front doors set in pairs rather than to the same side along a row as had been popular before.

Exterior Style

Despite trading all over the world we actually became a far more insular country in this period, looking to our own past for stylistic inspiration rather than to the Ancient World. The Gothic style purified by Pugin and ignited by Ruskin began to shape all sizes of house from the 1850s. Asymmetrical buildings, with steep pitched roofs, forward facing gables, pointed arches, and most notably, exposed brick with patterns of different colours, were a distinctive feature of the second half of the 19th century. The Classical style still battled for its own corner and Italianate, with distinctive flat roofs with bracketed eaves and semi-circular headed windows set in twos and threes, was popular in the middle of the century. Later, architects looked to old manor and farmhouses rather than medieval churches for inspiration, using mock timber framing, hanging tiles, and terracotta for decoration.

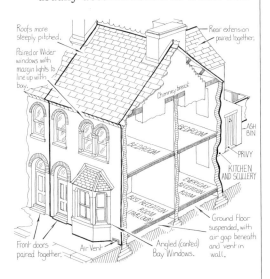

Victorian house structure: *A cut-away of a middle class terrace house showing some of the structural details which were typical during the second half of the 19th century.*

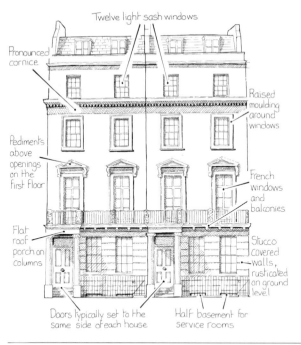

Twelve light sash windows

Pronounced cornice

Pediments above openings on the first floor

Flat roof porch on columns

Raised moulding around windows

French windows and balconies

Stucco covered walls, rusticated on ground level

Doors typically set to the same side of each house

Half basement for service rooms

Early Victorian terrace: *An early Victorian large terrace with labels of fashionable details of the time. Although they continued to be built in a similar style to the previous Regency examples, the four-panelled door had by now replaced the six as the standard form.*

Italianate style: *This was popular in the 1850s and 1860s after Queen Victoria's Osborne House had been completed in the style. Shallow pitched roofs with eaves supported on brackets and pairs of round-headed windows were elements which found their way onto ordinary terrace housing.*

Gothic style: *The pointed arch was one of the key elements of this revival of medieval architecture but its application to the mass of terrace housing was limited usually to the occasional front door or, as in this case, a window.*

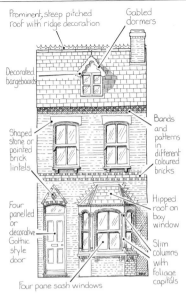

Prominent, steep pitched roof with ridge decoration

Gabled dormers

Decorated bargeboards

Shaped stone or pointed brick lintels

Bands and patterns in different coloured bricks

Four panelled or decorative Gothic style door

Hipped roof on bay window

Slim columns with foliage capitals

Four pane sash windows

Mid Victorian façade: *The front of a middle class terrace from the 1860s and 1870s with labels of some of its fashionable features. The repeal of the window tax and the widespread availability of cheap glass meant bays could now be fitted to this class of house, although they were usually just single storey at this date.*

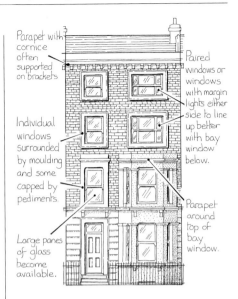

Parapet with cornice often supported on brackets

Paired windows or windows with margin lights either side to line up better with bay window below.

Individual windows surrounded by moulding and some capped by pediments.

Parapet around top of bay window.

Large panes of glass become available.

Mid Victorian Classical: *Elevation of a medium/large terrace house in a Classical style showing some of the key features from this period. Windows with thinner pieces either side were popular, to line up with the fashionable angled bays below.*

Ilam, Staffs: *Many villages were rebuilt with 'Olde English' style housing by landlords with half an eye on impressing their guests. This example from the 1850s, with decorative bargeboards, hanging tiles, and steep pitched roofs, gives a foretaste of the revival styles which became popular from the 1870s.*

Sash Window Box

Pulleys

Horns

Counter-weight

Mid Victorian sash window: *These usually had two panes in each sash or in the finest houses just a single one. Without the glazing bars the frame became weak so short protrusions below the centre bar called horns were added to make the joints stronger. Most windows at this time were painted a dark colour or grained to imitate a hardwood.*

Revival houses: *The next generation of architects, most notably Sir Richard Norman Shaw, who designed this building in the early 1870s, used 16th- and 17th-century houses for inspiration, with timber framing, brick or stone bases and prominent stacks of chimneys.*

Prominent chimneys.

Dutch and Flemish gables.

Upper window pane divided up.

White painted window frames and stonework.

Terracotta panels.

Carved brick lintels.

Tall square and angled bay windows.

Deep red brickwork.

Terracotta tile:
Terracotta plaques and tiles were a popular form of decoration on the exterior of late Victorian houses. The sunflower emblem used here was a favourite of Revival and Arts and Crafts designers.

Queen Anne façade: *By the 1880s Norman Shaw had popularised a new style based upon late 17th-century houses (not actually in the reign of Queen Anne), with Dutch gables, red brick, and white dressings and painted windows. The large pane sash window did not suit this Classical style so a compromise which was distinctive of late Victorian and Edwardian houses was to have the upper sash divided by glazing bars but the lower left as a single sheet so as not to block the view.*

Terracotta finials and ridge tiles

Patterns formed in the roof tiles

Large single panes of glass

Glass upper panels in door.

Outward facing gables and bargeboards.

Terracotta mouldings.

Deeply recessed doorways with tiled sides and floor.

Bay windows now popular on smaller houses.

Towers: *Towers and turrets at the end of terraces or detached houses, decorated bargeboards and hanging tiles were popular in the 1870s and 1880s.*

Spires on turrets and towers

Decorated ridge tiles and finials

Bargeboards

Hanging tiles

Late Victorian façade: *A middle class terrace from the 1880s with labels of fashionable details. Doors often had glazed upper panels, and were deeply recessed back into the house with tiles often flanking the side and the pathway up to it.*

Bricks: *By the end of the 19th century, fine quality machine-made bricks with sharp edges and a durable surface were being transported all over the country. As these were still more expensive than common bricks, only the façade was built with them and down the sides cheaper common bricks were used. English bond was also revived in these last few decades with its alternate courses of headers and stretchers.*

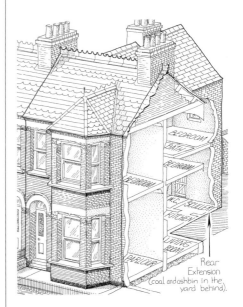

BEDROOM

BATH

BEDROOM

BEDROOM

BOX STAIRS

KITCHEN

LIVING ROOM

PARLOUR

Rear Extension (coal and ashbin in the yard behind).

Late Victorian terrace: *By the late Victorian period middle class homes could have full height bays, later examples of which were usually square sided rather than angled. Front doors were usually paired together and deeply recessed as in this example.*

Interior Style

Victorian interiors were more cluttered, bolder and colourful than before. Eclectic mixes of styles, scattered furniture and masses of ornaments and plants were often found. Mass production and the growth of magazines and shops meant the middle classes could imitate the luxurious fittings of their social superiors, and styles spread more rapidly across the country. The hierarchy of decoration still applied, impressing guests with the owner's refined taste, and meant that the hall, drawing and dining rooms were 'best' while upstairs out of sight the fittings became plain in comparison. Ceiling heights grew in most terraces, and floors were raised up so that an air gap existed below where there was no basement or cellar. Walls were plain early on with large skirting boards but later the dado and picture rails in various combinations made a come-back.

Victorian interior: *A mid-Victorian parlour with busy patterns, scattered furnishings and a mantelpiece packed with ornaments.*

Fireplace surrounds: *There was a wide range of styles from the Classical to the Gothic and in a variety of materials, including marble and hardwoods in the best rooms and simple cast iron or soft wood examples in bedrooms.*

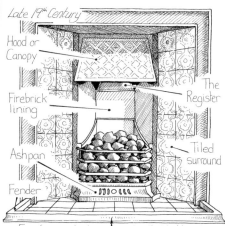

Fenders not always used with tiled hearth.

Grates: *Register grates came in various forms but the most distinctive are the semi-circular opening which was popular in the middle of the period and the later more refined example with tiled flanks to reflect more heat into the room.*

Hall: *The hall was important to Victorians as a means of impressing visitors. Ceramic tiled floors, dado rails and anaglypta wallpaper, and in some halls even a fireplace and chair for waiting guests, could be found.*

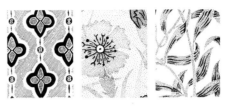

Wallpaper: *Mass production in the first half of the century meant that for the first time middle class houses could be decorated with wallpaper in an ever increasing range of designs. Busy patterns were replaced in the middle of the period with simple two-dimensional designs while, later in the period, lighter papers with highlighted floral patterns became popular.*

Newel post

String

Panelling

Closed String: balustrade rests on side string.

Stairs: *Although there was a wide variety of types, the decorative wooden closed string stair which had been common in the 17th century was a popular revival in this period.*

Bedroom: *Bedrooms were not only for sleeping in but also for dressing and washing oneself using a small basin and water brought up by servants. Bathrooms began to be standard fittings in middle class houses towards the end of the century, as staff became harder to find, and improved water pressure and drainage made the supply of running water up to the upper floor possible.*

Chapter ❼

Edwardian House Style

1900 - 1918

Edwardian semi-detached house: *One half of a large semi-detached house with popular features from the late Victorian and Edwardian periods, including patterned timber gables, casement windows with stained glass uppers, and a balcony with French windows. It impresses with its size, spacious grounds, and the quality and variety of its details.*

For all the pomp and ceremony, flamboyant Classically-styled public buildings and the image of lazy summers by the river, the Edwardian period was one of great social and political change which possibly would have been of more note had not the First World War intervened before it had borne its fruits. We had our first Prime Minister without a country seat, a Chancellor of the Exchequer who, through his budget, sought to spread the nation's wealth more evenly and create welfare schemes, and the first serious attempts to solve the problem of working class housing. Competitions and exhibitions were held, with the aim of producing cheaper houses so slums could be cleared out, a mission taken up by the First Garden City at Letchworth and various rural suburban developments. Most of these, however, became middle class havens, but the seeds had been sown which would be reaped at a later time.

Structure

The houses built in this period took shape in the 1890s and most were inspired by the work of architects from earlier than that. The spread of the suburban rail network and cheap train tickets meant middle class families could live further out of town on cheaper land, so that they could afford a larger house with a garden – the 'semi' had arrived. The working classes used trams and bicycles to escape the worst areas of town and those fortunate enough could afford small suburban terraces, perhaps even with their own privy. Most houses were now taller and deeper than a century before, the popularity of the garden on larger houses meaning that the rear of the house could have as much attention lavished upon it as the front.

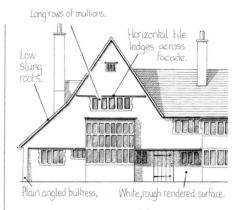

Long rows of mullions.

Horizontal tile ledges across facade.

Low slung roofs.

Plain angled buttress.

White, rough rendered surface.

Arts and Crafts houses: *A house designed by C.F.A. Voysey with labels of the distinctive Arts and Crafts features. Although it had been a social movement campaigning against industrialisation, the style which developed was popularised by magazines and leading shops and had decorative elements applied to the mass housing market.*

Garden suburbs: *A number of these developments were built in this period inspired by schemes like Port Sunlight, which is where this semi, clad in a wide variety of Arts and Crafts-style details like hanging tiles, pebbledash, mock timber framing and angled buttress, is from. These Edwardian developments, however, did little to empty the slums and became middle class havens.*

Exterior Style

The style of suburban housing was dominated by the earlier work of Revival architects like Norman Shaw and the Arts and Crafts movement. Pebbledashed walls, mock timber gables, hanging red tiles and terracotta decoration were popular on terraces of the time. Classical styles were once again fashionable, mainly on mansions and public buildings, but a revival of early 18th-century houses known as Neo Georgian began to appear. Art Nouveau, which had developed on the Continent, inspired in part by the Arts and Crafts movement, was treated with disdain by many in this still insular environment, but small pieces of its characteristic sinuous form appear in handles, tiles and stained glass which was popular at the time.

Revival styles:

A house influenced by the work of the Arts and Crafts movement and Revivalists like Sir Richard Norman Shaw, with labels of its distinctive parts. The architects who designed this house went on to plan Letchworth, the First Garden City, as many leading designers began turning their attention to working class housing problems.

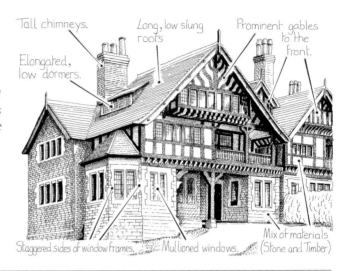

Tall chimneys.

Long, low slung roofs

Prominent gables to the front.

Elongated, low dormers.

Staggered sides of window frames.

Mullioned windows.

Mix of materials (Stone and Timber)

Prominent chimneys sometimes sited down the slope of the roof

Gables with mock timber framing

Window frames protrude from surface.

Fine cut brick lintels

Pebbledash

Casement windows with divided top section.

Continuous roof over bay and door.

Square bays

Medium sized terrace: *An elevation showing how Arts and Crafts style details like pebbledash, timber framing and stained-glass were applied to standard terrace housing. The continuous porch across the whole façade is distinctive of this period.*

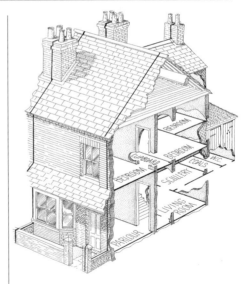

BEDROOM

CUPBOARD

BEDROOM

COALS

W.C.

BEDROOM

SCULLERY

LIVING ROOM

PARLOUR

Small sized terrace: *A cut-out of a modest sized terrace with a rear extension providing additional rooms. Although there was no bathroom, it had running water and an outside toilet. Edwardian houses usually had the chimney stack built directly above the fireplaces so it emerges halfway down the slope of the roof.*

Semi-detached house: *A cut-out of an Edwardian semi-detached house. It is on a wider plot so there is a more spacious hall and the kitchen is now fitted within the main body of the house.*

Doors and porches: *Doors with glass panels becoming smaller towards the top and various other arrangements were distinctive of the period. Porches were often highly decorative with white woodwork perforated with patterns and spindles.*

Stained glass: *This was popular in the upper panels of windows and in front doors. Patterns reflected Art Nouveau and Arts and Crafts fashions with stylized floral designs being most popular. The casement windows in this picture made a come-back in the late 19th century and began to replace sash windows although the latter were still widely fitted until the 1920s.*

Letchworth Garden City: *This First Garden City had tree-lined avenues and greens to bring the country into the city. The theme was continued with most houses inspired by the traditional English cottage, as in these examples featuring dormer and casement windows, rendered walls, low slung roofs and surrounded by hedges with picket gates.*

51

General interior:
An Edwardian drawing room with French doors to the garden, a display cabinet, fireplace with shelving for ornaments and a generally lighter atmosphere compared with earlier examples.

Interior Style

The fashion conscious Edwardian would have turned out the clutter and busy patterns of previous generations and made their interiors lighter, cleaner and uncluttered spaces to live in. Sunshine was brought into the house with paler coloured walls to reflect it. Fashionable decor from France, Japan and India was easier for middle classes to access through department stores, magazines and the Ideal Home Exhibition which began in 1908, and mass production made it affordable.

Despite this bright future the present was still a dirty place to live in with soot, grime and mud just outside the door. Strong colours, patterned papers and hygienic materials which wouldn't show the dirt were still used, especially in the hall.

Fireplace surrounds: *Examples of wooden Edwardian fireplaces. Additional shelving for ornaments either above or below the mantelpiece and mirrors built into the overmantel were common features. A chimney cloth was often hung from the mantelpiece, originally to keep smoke out of the room but by this date it was purely decorative.*

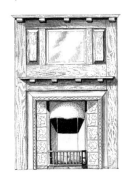

Art Nouveau details: *Although this foreign style was sometimes regarded with suspicion many decorative elements found their way into fashionable interiors. Its stylized floral and sinuous forms in the tiles on the fireplace are very distinctive. Designers in Scotland like Charles Rennie Mackintosh made more geometric forms of decoration, while Tiffany lamps from America with their stained-glass shades were popular.*

Arts and Crafts fireplace: *Large inglenook fireplaces with seating, shelves and cupboards were popular in the finest Arts and Crafts houses.*

Hall:

An Edwardian hallway with black and white tiled floor, relief paper covering the dado, and a simple patterned paper above this. The stairs have more room than in Victorian houses of this class and a decorative newel post and balustrade can now be fitted, with the door leading to the service rooms at the rear.

Wallpapers: *Examples of floral patterned wallpapers which could be found in late Victorian and Edwardian houses. Some were the work of leading designers including William Morris and C.F.A .Voysey, or others created by working anonymously for companies like the Silver Studio or shops such as Liberty.*

Chapter 8

1930s House Style

1918 - 1939

1930s detached house: *A typical detached house from the 1930s, brick-built, with round bay (bow) window, prominent gable, steep hipped roof and semi-circular porch set into the wall. It is red brick with machine-made tiles on the roof, with some hung from the gable and bay, and wooden casement windows. Its simple plan with a front and rear room, kitchen and three bedrooms above was repeated across the country.*

The inter-war years were turbulent and shocking, shaped by the catastrophe of the First World War, demands upon the Empire, and international financial problems, and characterised by outrageous fashions, music and art. In these short years much of the work done by previous generations to redress the balance of the nation's wealth started to take effect in bricks and mortar. Under pressure from the mass of returning soldiers, schemes like 'Homes Fit For Heroes' were the first attempts at a national programme of local authority housing, clearing slums and erecting spacious new houses. At the other end of the scale, inheritance tax, death duty, falling land values and the loss of heirs in the war crippled many aristocratic families; only a handful of large country houses were built and far more were sold to become schools or were even demolished.

Structure

Despite the turbulence of the financial markets, huge numbers of houses were built, mostly in the suburbs around the capital and those towns and cities in which new industries producing cars, electrical appliances and chemicals were based. Now large-scale building companies emerged and aided by government incentives and cheap land costs, they laid out estates with characteristic crescents and culs-de-sac flanked by square-planned semis. For the better off they could have large full height bow windows, a garage to the side and a flavour of the past with mock timber and pebbledash. Cheaper houses were plain in comparison but with the fields they were built on costing so little even these offered vastly more interior space and a front and rear garden compared with the terrace back in the old town centres.

Exterior Style

The influence of the architects who worked under the banner of the Arts and Crafts movement in the 1890s was still felt in this period. Builders took features and details from houses designed by Voysey, Baillie Scott and Lutyens and applied them to their standard plan box semi or detached house, as Mock Tudor, Neo Georgian and Pseudo Elizabethan houses were built all over the country. Modernist architecture, itself rooted in the edicts of Ruskin and Morris, appeared as occasional shocking white blocks amongst the mass of nostalgic homes. Hollywood films created a taste for the American streamlined version of Art

1930s semis: *Inter-war private housing estates were dominated by the semi-detached house and tree-lined crescents, avenues and culs-de-sac. These examples with curved bay windows and room for a garage differentiate them from cheaper housing, an important consideration for prospective owners.*

Moderne houses: *A row of semi-detached houses with Moderne features like sun-trap windows and a white rendered finish; yet underneath they are little different from those in the previous view. The various styles of the 1920s and 1930s house were often simply applied to a similar structure.*

Deco with distinctive sunray patterns and round-ended bays which put a fresh face upon the suburban semi.

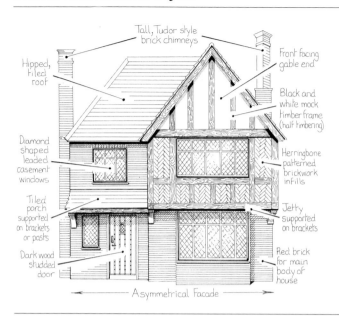

Tall, Tudor style brick chimneys

Hipped, tiled roof

Front facing gable end

Black and white mock timber frame (half timbering)

Diamond shaped leaded casement windows

Herringbone patterned brickwork infills

Tiled porch supported on brackets or posts

Jetty supported on brackets

Dark wood studded door

Red brick for main body of house

← Asymmetrical Facade →

Mock Tudor style: *A drawing of a Mock Tudor style house with labels of some of the distinctive features.*

High and Over, Amersham, Bucks: *It was a shock in 1930 to the residents of leafy Bucks to find this modern, stark white house rising above the trees. Its 'Y'-shaped plan was distinctive of the period but its reinforced concrete structure (although the walls were rendered brick) was more revolutionary.*

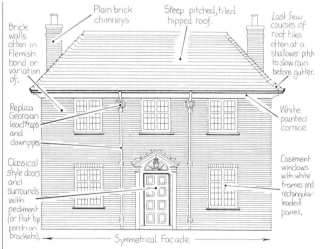

Plain brick chimneys

Steep pitched, tiled hipped roof.

Last few courses of roof tiles often at a shallower pitch to slow rain before gutter.

Brick walls often in Flemish bond or variation of.

Replica Georgian lead traps and downpipes

White painted cornice

Classical style doors and surrounds with pediment (or flat top porch on brackets).

Casement windows with white frames and rectangular leaded panes.

← Symmetrical Facade →

Neo Georgian style: *A Neo Georgian style house with labels highlighting some of the distinctive features.*

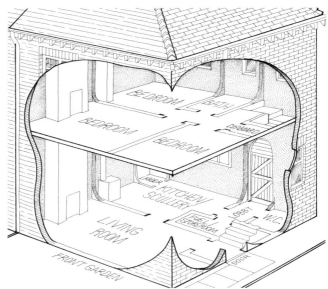

Council houses: *A semi-detached council house dating from the 1930s with a cut-away showing a possible interior layout and a side entrance. These sometimes huge council estates were tightly regulated and the houses were still too expensive for many to rent. Others found the strict regulations excessive and returned by choice to slum areas.*

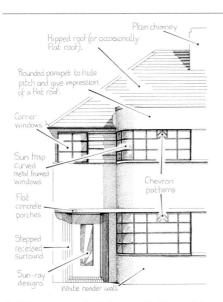

Plain chimney

Hipped roof (or occasionally Flat roof).

Rounded parapet to hide pitch and give impression of a flat roof.

Corner windows

Sun trap Curved metal framed windows

Chevron patterns

Flat concrete porches

Stepped recessed surround

Sun-ray designs

White render wall

Art Deco style: *A Moderne or Art Deco style house with labels highlighting some of the distinctive features. In this country what we now refer to generally as Art Deco was also known as Moderne, with an 'e' to differentiate it from more progressive modern architecture.*

Windows: *Casement windows with hinged openings replaced sash windows with either wooden or, later in the 1930s, metal frames. It was common for there to be a separate smaller upper window which was often patterned or filled with coloured glass designs to reflect the style of house (Art Deco in this case).*

Sunray pattern: *The sunray design was one of the most popular and was used on front gates and gables.*

Interior Style

Inter-war interiors were lighter and more spacious, sometimes fitted out with complete new room sets supplied by an expanding range of specialist furnishing and department stores. Exotic and nostalgic styles were designed to transport the owner to some far flung place or time to escape the grind and turmoil of urban life. Arts and Crafts, Mock Tudor and French Art Deco pieces were popular early on while, later, the distinctive streamlined version of the latter with curved furniture, bold geometric patterns and the sunray symbol may have been purchased by the most fashionable couples. It is likely that most made do with the existing pieces they had and mixed new with old.

1930s interior: *A notable change in 1930s houses was the shift of emphasis from the fireplace to the window or French doors, as light was one of the controlling factors in the design of Moderne interiors. An Art Deco interior like this, however, was beyond the reach of most and it is likely that homes were filled with an eclectic mix of traditional furniture, family heirlooms and the latest gadgets.*

Doors: *Internal door design changed from the traditional Victorian four-panelled type which was popular in the Edwardian house to one based on a single panel on the upper third and multiple vertical panels on the bottom section. In Moderne houses horizontal panels stacked one upon the other were popular, some examples with opaque or reeded glazing.*

  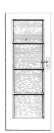

Fireplaces: *The most distinctive form of fireplace was the solid, stepped piece with dropped shoulders and glazed tile decoration with matching enamelled ashpans. In many houses, chimneys might have been dispensed with and electric fires fitted.*

  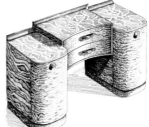 

Art Deco style: *Art Deco items were widely available for the 1930s house but usually in the form of light fittings, mirrors, tableware, clocks, and vanity ware. Earlier pieces used* ebony and bronze decoration inspired by Aztec and African art, while the distinctive geometric and streamline styles from America proved popular later.

Stairs: *With the wider hall a flight of stairs with a right-angle turn towards the bottom and an expanded lower step were often fitted, as in this example from a Moderne style house.*

Halls: *The hall of a semi-detached house was wider so a separate window to the side rather than a fanlight above the front door was fitted, now that ceiling heights were lower. Servants were very hard to find after the First World War so floors and walls, especially in the hall, had to be hygienic but patterned like this Art Deco design to hide the dirt.*

Glossary

Architrave: The moulding around a door, window or niche.

Area: Common name for the open space in front of a large terraced house down which steps lead to the basement.

Ashlar: Smooth, squared stone masonry with fine joints.

Baluster: Plain or decorated post supporting the stair rail. A balustrade is a row of balusters with a rail along the top.

Bargeboard: External vertical boards which protect the ends of the sloping roof on a gable and were often decorated.

Bay window: A window projecting from the façade of a house, of varying height but always resting on the ground.

Bonding: The way bricks are laid in a wall with the different patterns formed by alternate arrangements of headers (the short ends) and stretchers (the long side).

Bow window: A bay window with a bow-shaped (segmental arch) plan.

Capital: The decorated top of a Classical column.

Casement window: A window which is hinged along the side.

Cornice: A decorative moulding which runs around the top of an external or internal wall.

Dado: The lower section of a wall between the skirting and dado or chair rail.

Dormer: An upright window set in the roof and casting light into the attic rooms.

Eaves: The section of the roof timbers under the tiles or slates where they meet the wall, usually protected by a facia board.

Façade: The main vertical face of the house.

Fanlight: The window above a door, lighting the hall beyond, named after the radiating bars in semi-circular Georgian and Regency versions.

Gable: The pointed upper section of wall at the end of a pitched roof.

Glazing bars: The internal divisions of a window which support the panes.

Jambs: The sides of an opening for a door or window.

Keystone: The centre stone in an arch or lintel, often projected as a feature.

Lintel: A flat beam which is fitted above a door or window to take the load of the wall above.

Moulding: A decorative strip of wood, stone or plaster.

Mullion: A vertical member dividing a window.

Newel: The principal vertical post in a set of stairs.

Oriel: A projecting window supported from the wall rather than the ground.

Parapet: The top section of wall above the sloping end of the roof.

Pediment: A triangular or segmental arched feature supported by columns or pilasters.

Pilaster: A flat Classical column built out from a wall or fireplace and projecting slightly from it.

Pitch: The angle by which a roof slopes. A plain sloping roof of two sides is called a pitched roof.

Portico: A structure forming a porch over a doorway, usually with a flat cover supported by columns.

Quoins: The corner stones at the junction of walls. Often raised above the surface, made from contrasting materials or finished differently from the rest of the wall for decorative effect.

Render: A protective covering for a wall (see stucco).

Reveal: The sides (jambs) of a recessed window or door opening.

Rustication: The cutting of stone or moulding of stucco into blocks separated by deep incised lines and sometimes with a rough hewn finish. Often used to highlight the base of a Classical-styled house.

Sash window: A window of two separate sashes which slide vertically (or horizontally on smaller Yorkshire sash windows).

String: The side support panel for a staircase.

String course: A horizontal band running across a façade and usually projecting.

Stucco: A plaster which was used to render, imitate stonework, and form decorative features especially on Classical-styled houses.

Tracery: The ribs which divide the top of a stone window and are formed into patterns.

Transom: The horizontal bar in a window.

Vernacular: Buildings made from local materials in styles and methods of construction passed down within a distinct area, as opposed to architect-designed structures made from mass produced materials.

Voussoir: The wedge-shaped stones or bricks which make up an arch.

Wainscot: Timber lining of internal walls or panelling.

Time Chart

A time chart in horizontal strips, comprising architects, dates, period and styles, starting at 1530 in the top left and working down the page from left to right until 1930 at the bottom right.

Strip 1

Architects: Robert Smythson — Inigo Jones — / Robert Lyminge —

1530	1540	1550	1560	1570	1580	1590	1600	1610	1620

Period: TUDOR | ELIZABETHAN | JACOBEAN

Styles: TUDOR / RENAISSANCE (ELIZABETHAN PRODIGY HOUSE) (JACOBEAN PRODIGY HOUSES)

Strip 2

Architects: John Webb — / Hugh May — / Sir Roger Pratt — / William Talman / Sir John Vanbrugh / Nicholas Hawksmoor / Burlington / Colen Campbell / James Gibbs

1630	1640	1650	1660	1670	1680	1690	1700	1710	1720

Period: JACOBEAN | COMMONWEALTH | RESTORATION | WILLIAM + MARY / ANNE | GEORGIAN

Styles: RENAISSANCE (CAROLEAN) (DUTCH STYLE) BAROQUE

Strip 3

Architects: William Kent — / James Paine / Giacomo Leoni / John Carr / Robert Adam / Sir William Chambers / James Wyatt / Samuel Wyatt / George Steuart / Henry Holland / Sir John Soane / George Dance / John Nash / William Wilkins

1730	1740	1750	1760	1770	1780	1790	1800	1810	1820

Period: GEORGIAN | REGENCY

Styles: PALLADIAN NEO-CLASSICISM PICTURESQUE / GOTHIC / NEO-CLASSICISM + GREEK REVIVAL

Strip 4

Architects: Sir Charles Barry — / Sir Gilbert Scott — / Richard Norman Shaw — / A.W.N. Pugin / S.S. Teulon / Philip Webb — / John Dobson / C.R. Cockerell / Anthony Salvin — / Sir Edwin Lutyens —

1830	1840	1850	1860	1870	1880	1890	1900	1910	1920

Period: VICTORIAN | EDWARDIAN | WWI | MODERN

Styles: GOTHIC / ARTS + CRAFTS / TRADITIONALISTS / ITALIANATE / QUEEN ANNE / EDWARDIAN CLASSICISM

Index

Further Reading

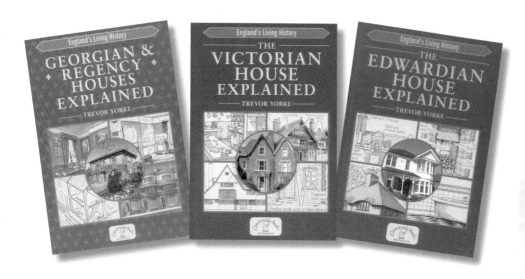